Hometown Favorites

What are you Craving?

Recipes from the Pie Dump

Recipes Collected and Refined by Mac and Cherie Munns
Compiled by Shandi Ditlevsen
Photos by Danielle Rieske

DEDICATED TO:
OUR LOYAL CUSTOMERS,
ALL OUR DEDICATED EMPLOYEES OVER
THE MANY YEARS,
AND ALL OUR FAMILY.
EACH DAY YOU WERE PRAYED FOR AND LOVED.
THANK YOU FOR BEING PART OF OUR EVERY DAY.

MAC AND CHERIE MUNNS

TABLE OF CONTENTS

6-7	The History
8-9	Dough
10-11	Bread
12-13	Hot Rolls
14-15	Scones
16-17	Potatoes and Gravy
18-29	Meats
30-39	Fried Foods
40-51	Sides
52-53	Soup
54-57	Cinnamon Rolls
58-63	Donuts
64-75	Desserts
76-85	Cookies
86-99	Pies
100-101	Slush

T. = Tablespoon   t. = Teaspoon

c. = Cup   lbs=Pounds

oz = Ounces

All Temperatures are in ° Fahrenheit.

2022 marked 100 years since The Pie Dump opened and started treating loyal customers to staple items such as their famous hot rolls and gravy and donuts. H.E. Grant opened the doors for business in 1922. In 1925, R.A. Christensen bought The Pie Dump and this is when it really got its name. R.A.'s wife would make over 50 pies a day and the students would run over to be the first in line.

About 3 years later, Leland Hansen decided it sounded like fun to run a restaurant. He bought the business, added selling pies from the school bus he drove, and added a book store. They also added candy bars and said that because it was something new to customers, the candy sold the very best.

Donna and Gordan Worley purchased The Pie Dump in 1944. They made donuts on a wood stove and it was now that the famous hot rolls, potatoes, and gravy came into play. Many people remember Donna's chocolate cake and soft ice cream. The first year Worley's were in business Cherie's dad(Boyd Marble) spent his summer earnings at The Pie Dump. Mac and Cherie also ate there in high school and the Worley's catered their wedding. Donna and Gordan named it Worley's Sweet Shoppe, but everyone in the valley still called it The Pie Dump. Never in a million years did Mac and Cherie anticipate that this would be where they would raise their family and earn their livelihood.

In 1982, they were given the opportunity to run and later buy Worley's Sweet Shoppe. The first year, they ran it with Dee, Cherie's brother, and his wife Kari. They kept the name Sweet Shoppe, dropped the Worley's, and added Munns's, but the people of the valley still called it The Pie Dump.

In 1994, they remodeled, but two years later they almost had to close the doors. With the influx of 15 fast food restaurants in the Bear River Valley, it was hard to compete. They had done well on hot rolls, potatoes and gravy, but now was the time to rethink the menu. So with some much needed education, they added a little bit of everything as daily specials and it worked! They would live to cook again! This was the year they added pies, using Cherie's mom's pie crust recipe. They baked 350 pies the day before Thanksgiving! Very fitting for a place called The Pie Dump.

In 2002, Mac went to work at Chanshare Sod Farm for a bit. Their son Zachary and his wife ran Munns's Sweet Shoppe for 2 years while Cherie had her knees replaced. That year was the first year The Pie Dump was open for the summer.

In February 2004, Mac decided it was time to return to the life he loved; baking, telling jokes, and enjoying people and Cherie came along for the ride.

At this time, they did a major renovation and added a steak house as part of the business. They became, The Pie Dump by Day/-TL Steak House by Night with the Motto "You are our future!" Catchy name since customers, who always know best, continued to call it The Pie Dump. The steak house went very well for 5 years, but when the recession hit in 2009, there was such a decline in business that they had to close it's doors. The Pie Dump continued, a place that always seemed to hold its own.

So it became The Pie Dump / -TL Catering. A mouth-watering breakfast menu was added and for the first time ever opened on Saturday morning for breakfast from 7 to 12. They catered everything you can imagine, on and off site, day or night.

One highlight was when Guy Fieri came with Diners, Drive-ins, and Dives. He loved the food! No surprise there!

The Pie Dump evolved over the years because their customers asked them to. The loyal customers were the ones that made the Pie Dump an icon in the community for 100 years.

WHITE BREAD DOUGH

2 1/4 c. Warm Water

2 T. Sugar

1 T. Yeast

1 1/2 t. Salt

1 T. Canola Oil or your oil of choice

3/4 c. Sour Dough Start*

1 egg

2 T Dough Conditioner**

6 1/2 c. High Gluten Flour***

Set aside 2 cups of flour. Mix the water, sugar, yeast, salt, oil, sour dough start, and egg. Add 4 1/2 c of the flour and mix for 3 minutes. Add in the other 2 cups of flour. Dough should pull away from the sides of the bowl, but still stick a little to the bottom. Depending on elevation and weather, you may need to add more flour or water until the dough starts to pull away from the sides of the bowl. You can mix in your mixer or knead by hand for 8 minutes. Cover and let the dough double in size.

*If you do not have Sour Dough Start, you can leave it out, but you may need to adjust measurements on flour. Also, depending on how thick or liquid your start is, it may need a little adjusting.

**Scratch Premium Dough Conditioner can be found on Amazon and some specialty kitchen stores.

**High gluten flour contains the highest amount of protein among wheat flours, at 12.5–14.5% — bread flour contains 12–14% and all-purpose flour contains 8.7–11.8%. Try to use the highest protein flour that you have available to you.

This dough is the base for many of the following recipes.
It will make 2 loaves of Bread(page 11), 1 dozen Hot Rolls(page 13), 1 dozen Cinnamon Rolls(page 54), or 2 Dozen Donuts(page 58).

HISTORY: This recipe has changed and evolved over the years. For the first 20 years it was measured in scoops of flour and about this much of this and that. To this day, if you ask Mac for a recipe it is,"About this much of this and that until it feels or looks right". As others came in to work, they needed to nail down a more concrete recipe and this recipe was established, but in 16 times the quantity.

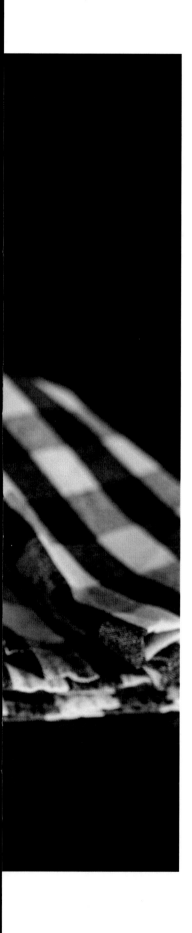

BREAD

Make a Batch of Dough from page 8.

1 Batch will make 2 loaves

Once your dough has doubled in size, pour it out on a floured surface and split the dough into 2.

Start to roll up the dough, tucking in the sides to keep the length of your bread pan. Then place dough in your lightly oiled bread pan.

Allow the dough to raise again, until you are an inch or 2 above the pan.

Preheat oven to 350°

Bake for 30 minutes. Or until the internal temperature is 190°.

Butter top immediately after removing it from the oven.

It is best to wait until bread is completely cool to cut into it, but sometimes it it just too tempting to cut a slice off the end and enjoy it warm with a bit of butter!

History: They almost always had loaves of bread at the Pie Dump, because whatever dough couldn't be made into hot rolls, got shaped and made into bread. They rarely sold loaves of bread though, so frequently Cherie would drop loaves off to friends and neighbors on her way home from work!

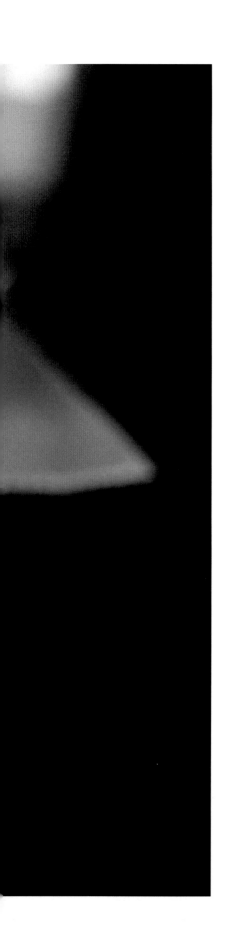

HOT ROLLS

Make a Batch of Dough from page 8.

Once your dough has doubled in size, you will start measuring individual hot rolls. Heavily oil your pan with melted butter/ oil of choice or as they used at the Pie Dump pork lard.

Each roll should weigh 4.5 oz. Stretch the dough over itself to smooth the top, then pinch the bottom. You will place 12 of them 3x4 in a 9x13 pan. As you are placing them, roll the tops around in the oil and then flip them over.

If you would like the crease down the center, take a metal spatula and press down until you hit the bottom of the pan on each individual roll.

Cover with a tea towel until they have raised an inch above the pan.

Preheated oven to 350 ° Bake for 40 minutes. (Cherie likes to rotate pans half way through) Until the internal temp is 190° Immediately brush the tops with butter after removing them from the oven.

History: At the Pie Dump they would place 1-2 T of Margarine inside the rolls. They tried to switch over to butter multiple times, but it changed the flavor and people noticed! So place whatever you would like inside, but know that at the Pie Dump; they used Margarine.

SCONES

Make a Batch of Dough from page 8.

Once your dough has doubled in size, roll out your dough to 1/2 in thick.

Cut circles with a wide mouth quart jar.

Allow them to raise for 20 minutes. They should double in size.

Heat oil to 350°

Gently work the dough with your hands until it is 1/3 larger.

Fry until the bottom is golden brown. Flip and wait for the other side to get golden brown.

Enjoy Hot and Fresh!

HONEY BUTTER

1/2 c. Butter-Room Temperature

3 T. Honey

Beat it together until it is fluffy.

History: Each Halloween Mac and Cherie's family would fry scones over an open fire for anyone that came by Trick or Treating. Everyone loved them and each year they would cook about 400 scones. Parents especially made sure it was on the trick or treating route! While the Steakhouse was open, they would serve them to anyone who came in and wanted one.

MASHED POTATOES

4 Baker Potatoes

1/2 c. Milk or Cream

1/4 c. Butter

1 t. Salt

Chop the potatoes and boil them until they fall apart when poked with a fork.

Drain off water.

Add Milk/Cream, Butter, and Salt.

Mash until desired consistency is achieved.

BROWN GRAVY

4 c. Water

4 t. Better than Bouillon Roasted Beef Base

4 T of Flour

1 c. Water

Bring the water and Bouillon to a boil.

Whisk Flour and Water together in a separate bowl.

Add to Broth and continue to whisk as it thickens.

WHITE GRAVY

1 lb of Sausage

6 heaping T of Flour

1/2 gallon Milk

Brown Sausage. Add Flour. Stir.

Slowly pour milk and whisk until it thickens.

At the Pie Dump it was lighter on the sausage, and they would use a full gallon of milk.

History: At the Pie Dump they went through different phases and for a time they actually used instant potatoes. But they returned to making a homemade mashed potatos. As they started to do more breakfast items on the grill; they also started doing grilled potato cakes. They put them into the breakfast burritos or they were also served as a side with some breakfast plates.

HOW TO COOK A STEAK

Allow the Steak to come to room Temperature.
Season the Steak heavily with the Steak Seasoning.
Use a well seasoned pan and get it to smoke point.
Place steak on the skillet and get a good sear. This helps seal in all the juices.
Flip and sear the other side.
Cook until you reach your desired doneness.

Rare: 120-125°
Medium Rare: 130-135°
Medium: 140-145°
Medium Well: 150-155°
Well: 160-165°

Be sure to allow your steak to rest for 5-10 minute.
If you cut into it too soon, the juices will run out and the steak may dry out.

STEAK SEASONING

4 T. Salt
2 T. Black Pepper
2 T. Garlic Powder*

Mix it up and put it in a cute little shaker to put on steaks, burgers, roasts, etc.

*If you are using granulated garlic, double the amount.

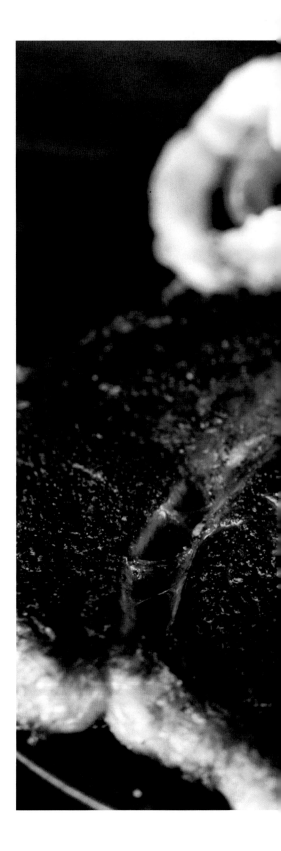

TURKEY TENDERS

5 lbs of Chicken Tenderloins
1 c. Soy Sauce
1 c. Citrus Flavored Soda
1 c. Oil of Choice
1/2 T. Garlic
1/2 T. Horseradish

Marinate for 6 hours or overnight. The longer you let them marinate the stronger the flavor will become. These are great to cook on the grill or in a skillet. Cook until internal temperature reaches 165°
Makes 15 Servings

History: They originally started making these with turkey, because at the time turkey was cheaper than chicken. But when turkey prices rose, they switched to chicken and left the name of Turkey Tenders.

ROAST BEEF

4 lb Roast

Cover the Roast Liberally with Steak Seasoning from page 18.

Cook at 400° for 1 hr.

Add water until half of the roast is under water.

Cover with Aluminum Foil/Lid and cook at 350° for 3 more hours.

This will produce a well done tender roast. Internal Temperature should be 160°

Save the juices for your brown gravy or if you want au jus to make a French dip!

Makes 12 servings

HORSERADISH SAUCE

1/2 c. Mayonnaise

1/2 c. Miracle Whip

1/2 c. Sour Cream

3 T. Horseradish

Mix well and Enjoy with the Roast Beef or a Steak.

History: As they started to do more and more catering, Roast Beef was one of the most popular items. Whether it was thin sliced for a French dip sandwich or a thicker cut for a dinner slice.

ROAST TURKEY

Cover entire turkey breast liberally with Salt and Poultry
Seasoning.
Cook at 400° for 1 hr.
Add water until half of the roast is under water.
Cover with Aluminum Foil/Lid.
Drop your heat to 350° and cook for 3 more hours.
The thickest part should have an internal temperature of 165°.

History: If you ask Mac and Cherie if they miss the Pie Dump,
they will tell you that they miss the people! Mac was always
prepared with a joke to tell, whether it was appropriate was
another story. One thing he frequently said, "I was doing good 'til
I seen you. (pause) Now I'm doing real good!" Catches most
people off guard, but he only teases the people he loves.
Cherie was always so welcoming and would lend a listening ear,
if anyone needed it. Before the remodel, there was a large
window in the back, that she would work at and those that knew
her, would go back there to chat and to get their orders.

RIBS

Preheat Oven to 400 °

Season your Rack of Ribs heavily with the steak seasoning from page 18 and Lemon Pepper. Place on a standard cookie sheet and bake for 1 hour. Cover with aluminum foil and drop the temperature to 350° and bake for another hour. Brush with your BBQ sauce of your choice.

History: At the steakhouse they would serve the ribs without any BBQ sauce on them, but would include a brush and 2-3 different kinds of BBQ sauce so you could choose the sauce of your choice. There was usually a spicy and a sweet one.

MANDARINE CHICKEN

2 lbs Chicken cut into thin strips

Batter

2 Eggs

1 c. Cornstarch

1/4 t. Salt

1/4 t. Garlic

Beat together until smooth.

Heat oil to 325°

Dip Chicken in Batter and fry until lightly browned.

Internal temperature should be 160°.

Sauce

1/4 c. Water

1/2 c. White Vinegar

3/4 c. Brown Sugar

Dash of Salt

2 c. Ketchup

2 T. Cornstarch

Put all ingredients in a sauce pan and whisk together until sauce thickens.

History: This was a recipe that was only ordered for catering and people only ordered it for special holidays like Easter, Christmas, and Thanksgiving. It was something the Munns Family had on special occasions, so it always felt a little extra special.

FRENCH FRIES

4 Russet Potatoes

Wash and cut potatoes into 1/4 inch strips.

You can peel them, if you prefer.

Soak in a bowl of cold water for 30 minutes.

Drain the water and put 3 heaping T. of Cornstarch and toss until they are coated in Cornstarch.

Heat Oil to 350°

Prefry for 3.5 minutes, then remove them.

Let them rest for at least 10 minutes or up to an hour. This allows the inside of the fry to finish cooking and make it nice and soft on the inside.

Then final fry for 7 minutes. This will crisp them up!

Makes 8 servings.

TARTAR SAUCE

1/2 c. Mayonnaise   1/2 c. Miracle Whip

1 t. Mustard   2 T. Chopped Onion

3 T. Dill Pickle Relish

Mix Well!

History: You may be wondering why we are putting the recipe for Tartar Sauce with the Fries!? Isn't tartar sauce usually served with fish? In the 80's the menu was fairly small and the high school students started mixing items to create something new. It was then, that a large fry with tartar sauce and brown gravy became one of the favorite items to order for the high school students. It may sound strange; and yes it is unique, but it is Delicious!

ONION RINGS

2 Large Yellow Onions

Batter

2 eggs

1 c. Milk

2 c. Flour

1 t. Salt

1 t. Pepper

1 1/2 t. Baking Powder

Slice Onions 1 inch thick and separate into individual rings. Coat generously in batter and fry in 350° oil until golden brown. Salt as soon as you remove them from the oil. Enjoy with fry sauce or Cherie prefers just ketchup.

FRY SAUCE

1/2 c. Mayonnaise

1/2 c. Miracle Whip

1/4 c. Ketchup

1/2 t. Mustard

Mix well!

History: These were one of the best selling appetizers at the Steakhouse!
When they remodeled and added the back room for the steakhouse, it was previously an apartment. It was actually where Mac and Cherie lived when they first got married. The floors back there are still the originals.

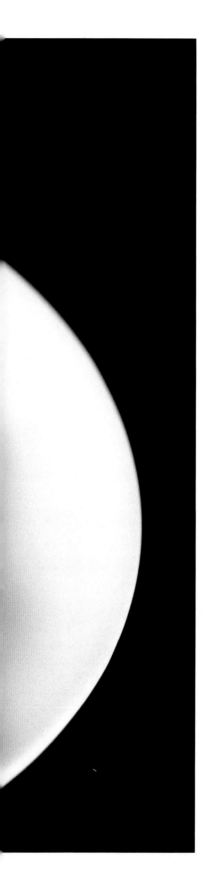

BATTERED MUSHROOMS

8 oz. Mushrooms
2 Eggs
1 c. Milk
2 c. Flour
1 t. Salt
1 t. Pepper
1 1/2 t. Baking Powder

Heat oil to 350°.
Whisk all the ingredients together.
Dip Mushrooms in the batter and gently lower into the oil. You may need to turn so that all sides turn golden brown.
Once they are all golden brown, remove them from the oil and salt.
At the Steakhouse we served these with Cocktail Sauce!

COCKTAIL SAUCE

1 c. Ketchup
1 T. Horseradish
Mix well!
Every bottle of horseradish varies a little on heat, so if it doesn't have enough kick, add a little more horseradish.

CHICKEN STRIPS

2 lbs of Chicken Tenderloins or Sliced Breast
Flour
Bread Crumbs

Milk Mixture
6 T. Milk
2 Eggs
1 t. Paprika
1 t. Steak Seasoning(pg18)

You will need to prepare 3 bowls; plain flour, milk mixture, and plain bread crumbs.
Preheat your oil to 350°
Dip your chicken into the milk mixture, flour, milk mixture, then bread crumbs. Fry for 3-8 minutes. Time will depend on the thickness of your chicken. The best way to know it is done, is to make sure the thickest part has an internal temperature of 165°.

History: Up until about 2008 they purchased Chicken Strips from Sysco and they were fine. They sold a TON of them to High School Students. But then they started breading them in house and they were what customers preferred!
YUMMY!

Coconut Shrimp

8 Shrimp

Milk Mixture

6 T. Milk	2 Eggs
1 t. Paprika	1 t. Steak Seasoning

Coconut Mixture

1 c. Bread Crumbs

1 c. Coconut

Clean and Fillet Shrimp(slice into shrimp from end to tail along the back curve, but not all the way through).

Preheat your oil to 325°

Dip your shrimp into the milk mixture, flour, milk mixture, then Coconut crumbs. Then fry for 3-5 minutes, until golden brown.

Sauces

1/4 c. Orange Marmalade	1/2 c. Honey Yogurt
1/4 small Jalapeño Finely Diced	1/2 c. Crushed
with no white or seeds	Pineapple

History: These are 2 different sauces that they served with the shrimp. If you want something with a kick, go for the jalapeño marmalade. Or for something sweet, go with the pineapple yogurt. Cherie's parents, Boyd and Cheryl Marble, loved these! When they would come into the Steakhouse Mac would start an order as soon as soon as they would walk in! We photographed it on an American Flag cutting board, because they were the most patriotic people you would ever meet!

Dutch Oven
Potatoes

4 lbs of Raw Potatoes
2 Medium Onions
1/2 c. Water
1/2 c. Citrus Flavored Soda
8 Slices of Bacon

Combine Potatoes, Onions, Water, and Soda.
Add Salt and Pepper.
Place the Raw Bacon on top so it browns.
Bake at 350° for 2 hours.
After 1 hour check to see if the bacon is crispy. If it
is, stir it into the potatoes, so it doesn't burn.
Makes 16 servings

History: As they started developing the menu for the Steakhouse, they had the idea to do the Dutch Oven potatoes and they were a huge hit! It was the most popular potato side requested.

BAKED BEANS

1 lb Ground Beef

1 Medium Onion Chopped

1 lb of Bacon

2-15 oz cans of Lima Beans

2-15 oz cans of Pork and Beans

2-15 oz cans of Kidney Beans; drained

1 c. Brown Sugar

1 c. Ketchup

1 t. Mustard

Preheat oven to 350°

Cook Bacon and Chop.

Brown Ground Beef with Onion.

Combine all the ingredients and Bake for 45 minutes.

Makes 15 Servings

History: This recipe came from Mac's Sister-in-law Beryl. Every summer at the family reunion she would make these and they were always a big hit! When they started the steakhouse, they offered it as a side and those they like baked beans, loved them! Before they closed in 2010 they tried to offer some lower priced items and Mac created a Baked Bean Burger that featured these, bacon, and fried cheese on their homemade buns. It was so delicious!

CINNAMON APPLES

5 Granny Smith Apples
1/3 c. Brown Sugar
2 T. Butter
2 t. Cinnamon

Peel and Slice Apples. Place all the ingredients in a skillet and cook over Medium/High Heat until the apples are to your desired tenderness.

History: As they were developing the menu for the Steakhouse, their children insisted that they garnish every skillet with this deliciousness. Employees loved to eat these with a scoop of ice cream and little of the caramel sauce(pg74). It was like a little Caramel Apple Pie a la mode without the crust.

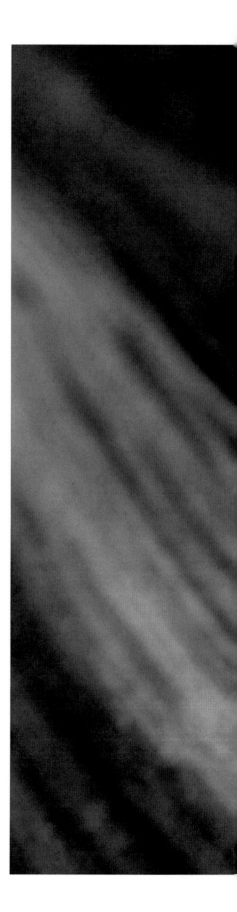

POTATO SALAD

4 Small Potatoes

3 Large Hard Boiled Eggs

1/2 c. Sweet Pickle Relish

1 T. Onion-Diced

1 c. Mayonnaise or Miracle Whip

1 T. Mustard

1 t. Sugar

1/2 t. Salt

1/4 t. Pepper

Boil Potatoes whole for 20 minutes. Poke with a fork half way in. If it goes in easily, it is done.

HOW TO BOIL EGGS

Cover your eggs in cold water* in a sauce pan, then put it on the heat.

When it comes to a boil, boil for 3 minutes.

Turn the heat off and put a lid on the pan. Let them sit for 20 minutes.

Dump off the hot water and run cold water over them for 3 minutes. Dump all the water off and shake them in the pan. Generally the peels will start to fall off. Peel under cold water. Make sure the membrane between the shell and the egg is completely removed. Allow to cool completely.

Dice potatoes and eggs.

Mix together Relish, Onion, Mayo, Mustard, Sugar, Salt, and Pepper.

Gently fold into potatoes and eggs.

Makes 8 Servings

*If you are using farm fresh eggs add 1 t. Soda to the water.

PASTA SALAD

2 c. Tricolored Pasta
1/4 c. Cauliflower
1/4 c. Broccoli
1/4 c. Carrots
1/4 c. Cucumber
1/2 c. Zesty Italian Dressing
1 t. Sugar

Cook pasta as instructed on the box.
Chop Cauliflower, Broccoli, Carrots, and Cucumber.
Once pasta is cooled, add all the vegetables, Italian Dressing and
Sugar.
Makes 6 servings.

History: In the earlier years, before any improvements or remodeling was done, they would have massive water fights on the last day of school. The entire floor would be covered in water and students would even climb up on the roof and dump buckets of water off the roof on to students trying to enter. Employees and students alike, were all soaked at the end of the day!

MACARONI SALAD

2 c. Elbow Macaroni
1 1/2 c. Cucumbers
1 1/2 c. Roma Tomatoes
2 T Chopped Onion
1 c. Miracle Whip or Mayonnaise
1 t. Sugar
1/2 t. Salt
1/2 t. Pepper

Cook Macaroni as instructed on the box.
Cut your Cucumbers into quarters, remove all the seeds, and then chop.
Chop the Tomatoes and Onion.
Mix the Miracle Whip/Mayo, Onion, Sugar, Salt, and Pepper.
Add in Macaroni, Cucumbers, and Tomatoes.
Makes 8 servings.

History: This recipe was Mac's Mother Eleanor's recipe. She passed away when he was only 16, so it is a beloved recipe that reminds him of her. His older brother remembers that sometimes she would put a can of shrimp in it, so if you enjoy canned shrimp, give that a try.

Chicken Noodle Soup

Noodles

2 c. Flour   1/2 t. Salt

2 Egg Yolks   1 whole Egg

1/3 c. Water   1 t. Olive Oil

Mix Flour & Salt in a bowl. Make a well. In a separate bowl combine Eggs, Water, & Oil.

Add wet ingredients into the well. Mix until it has just come together.

Flour your kneading surface. Turn the dough out and knead it until the dough is smooth and elastic. (8-10 minutes)

Allow to sit for 10 minutes.

Divide dough into 4 portions. Roll out into about a 12 inch square. It should be about 1/8 inch thick. Lightly flour and roll into to a jelly roll and cut unto 1/4 inch strips. Do the same with the other 3 portions.

Let them dry over night, or until they are completely dry.

Once they are dry you can store them in an air tight container in the fridge for 3 days.

Soup

1 Small Chicken

1 1/2 gallon of Water

2 T. Steak Seasoning

Simmer for 90 minutes.

Take the chicken out and let it and the stock completely cool. Remove all the chicken from the bones and remove the extra fat from the top of the chicken stock.

Bring the stock back to a boil.

Add 1/4 c. Pearl Barley and boil for 15 minutes.

Add 6 Medium Carrots-chopped and Boil for 5 Minutes.

Add

1 small Onion-diced

2 stalks of Celery-chopped

4 Medium Potatoes-cubed

Boil for 10 minutes

Add your Homemade Noodles and cook for another 4 minutes.

Add the chicken pieces.

Makes 16 Servings.

CINNAMON ROLL

Make a batch of dough from page 8.
Once your dough from page 8 has doubled in size, dump the dough out onto a floured surface and roll into a rectangle about 12 in x 18 in. Make sure the dough is not sticking to your counter and relaxes back into that size.
Put 1/2 c. of room temperature butter over the entire space. *Do not melt the butter.
Add 1 c. of Brown Sugar and
5 t. Cinnamon.
Roll up the dough along the 12 inch side.
Cut slices 1 inch thick. You should get 12 cinnamon rolls.
Heavily butter 2-9x13 pans and 6 will fit in each pan. Be sure to brush butter between each roll.
Cover with a tea towel and let double in size.
Preheat oven to 375°.
Bake for 20-25 minutes until golden brown on top.
Butter the tops.

FROSTING

1/3 c. Butter   4 1/2 c. Powdered Sugar
1/2 c. Milk   1 1/2 t. Vanilla
Beat together until smooth.
Wait until the Cinnamon Rolls are completely cool to frost, otherwise it will melt into the Cinnamon Roll.
Unless you want to eat them warm!

History: Some people liked their Cinnamon Rolls rewarmed a bit and would request them microwaved. Cherie liked hers right out of the oven, no frosting, eaten from the middle out. As they started doing a full breakfast on the grill, they would make French toast with day old Cinnamon rolls, cut in half, and it was a huge hit!

PUMPKIN SPICE ROLL

Follow the same instructions for the Cinnamon Rolls, but instead of Butter use 1-15 oz can of Pumpkin Puree and
5 t. of Pumpkin Pie Spice.

ORANGE ROLLS

Follow the same instructions for the Cinnamon Rolls. Add the 1/2 c of room temperature butter and then mix the zest from 2 oranges into 2 cups sugar and spread onto the dough.

CREAM CHEESE FROSTING

8 oz Softened Cream Cheese
1 1/2 t. Vanilla
3 c. Powdered Sugar
Beat together. Add up to 2 T of Milk to achieve spreading consistency.

History: During the Holidays the Pumpkin Spice Cinnamon Rolls were a huge hit and most people requested cream cheese frosting. Every Christmas the Munns Family would make Mini Orange Rolls for Christmas morning. They are perfect to make Christmas Eve and refrigerate. Then just let them rise and bake Christmas morning.

How to Make Donuts

Make a Batch of Dough from page 8.

Once your dough has doubled in size, roll out to 1 inch thick on a floured surface. Lift the dough and let it relax after rolling, otherwise your donuts will shrink.

Cut donuts using a donut cutter.

To make sweet rolls, use a pizza cutter to cut 2" by 5" rectangles.

If you would like a twist, cut your sweet rolls down the center, leaving 1/2" connected and then twist them together.

For bismarks, you can use a wide mouth mason jar.

Cover with a tea towel and allow them all rise to double the size.

Heat your oil to 350°

Gently lower the donut in to the oil and wait until it turns golden brown. Then turn and let the opposite side brown.

Immediately place your hot donuts in the frosting or glaze as desired. Let it sit for 2-3 minutes and then remove.

If you are adding breadcrumbs to your sweet rolls, immediately dip in crumbs from page 61.

Glaze

1 c. Powdered Sugar
1/4 c. Water
1/2 t. Vanilla
1/2 t. Salt

Whisk everything together. Add 1 t. of water at a time until it is at a drizzle consistency. At the Pie Dump they had a space set up to dump glaze over them and let them drip off. But we would suggest dipping and flipping at home.

CHOCOLATE FROSTING

1/3 c. Butter

4 1/2 c. Powdered Sugar

1/2 c. Milk

1 1/2 t. Vanilla

1/2 c. Dark Cocoa Powder

Mix together and place in a shallow pan, like a cake pan. The frosting will appear too thick, but it is the consistency you want to dip hot donuts in!

MAPLE FROSTING

1/3 c. Butter

4 1/2 c. Powdered Sugar

1/2 c. Milk

1 1/2 t. Vanilla

1 1/2 t. Crescent Maple Flavoring

Mix together and place in a shallow pan, like a cake pan. The frosting will appear too thick, but it is the consistency you want to dip hot donuts in!

BREAD CRUMBS

2 c. Bread Crumbs

1 t. Cinnamon

You can purchase bread crumbs or just cube some bread you have on hand and bake it for 2 hours at 200° until it is completely dry. Then throw it into your blender. Pulse until it is broken down. Go ahead and add the cinnamon and pulse it a few more times. Then place it in a shallow pan, like a cake pan, for dipping.

BISMARK

You will fry these up just like the donuts, but do not dip these in frosting. You will take chopstick or the end of a wooden spoon and poke a hole in one end and then hollow out the inside of the bismark.
After you have hollowed it out, allow it to cool completely, before filling it.
While it is cooling you can prepare your Filling.

FILLING

2 c. Heavy Whipping Cream
2 c. Vanilla Pudding

Whip Cream until it is Stiff and do not add any sweetener. Fold into the Vanilla Pudding. Put into a piping bag to fill Bismarks. Place in the refrigerator until Bismarks are completely cool.
Once they have cooled, fill them and then frost them with the Chocolate Frosting from page 61.

History: In later years they started making all kinds of specialty Bismarks and you can really play with what you fill them with.
Add some crushed oreos to the filling and on the frosting and you have a cookies and cream Bismark.
The Raspberry Bismark was filled with Raspberry jam with cream cheese frosting on top from page 57.

LEMON BARS

1 Lemon Cake Mix
1 Egg
1/3 c. Butter-Room Temperature

Mix together until crumbly.
Put 1/2 on the bottom of a 9x13 pan.
Bake at 350° for 15 minutes.
Let cool for 10 minutes.

8 oz Cream Cheese
1/3 c. Sugar
1 t. Lemon Juice
1 Egg

Beat it Cream Cheese, Sugar, Lemon Juice, and
Egg together.
Spread over the bottom layer.
Sprinkle remaining crumble on top.
Bake another 15 minutes.

History: When they started to cater more desserts, they started to offer more bars, because it was easier to bake a large sheet of them and then just cut them up. It was more cost effective for customers as well, because they were not as time intensive as individual cookies.

CARAMEL BROWNIES

1 German Chocolate Cake Mix

1 Egg

1/4 c. Room Temperature Butter

Carmel Sauce from page 74

1 c. Chocolate Chips

Preheat Oven to 350°.

Mix Cake Mix, Egg, and Butter together. It will be Crumbly.

Put 1/2 of the mixture in a 9x13 in pan and bake for 6 minutes.

Make a batch of the Carmel Sauce from page 74.

Sprinkle Chocolate Chips all over on the Crust.

Then pour your caramel sauce over.

Last you will sprinkle the other half of the cake crumble on top.

Bake for 20 minutes.

Coconut Bars

Crust

1 c. Butter-Room Temperature

2 c. Flour

1/2 c. Sugar

1/2 c. Corn Starch

1/4 t. Salt

Preheat oven to 350°

Mix all ingredients together. Put into a 9x13 pan. Bake for 10 minutes.

Filling

4 Eggs

2 c. Brown Sugar

1/2 t. Baking Powder

1 T. Flour

2 t. Vanilla

2 c. Walnuts

2 c. Coconut

Mix together and spread over crust.

Bake for 20 minutes.

Cream Cheese Frosting

3 T. Butter-Room Temperature

3 oz. Cream Cheese-Room Temperature

2 1/2 c. Powdered Sugar

1 t. Vanilla

Cream Butter and Cream Cheese together. Add Powdered Sugar and Vanilla. Spread on top once they have cooled completely.

PUMPKIN ROLL

3 Eggs
1 c. Sugar
2/3 c. Pumpkin Puree
1 t. Lemon Juice
1/2 t. Salt
3/4 c. Flour
1 t. Baking Powder
2 t. Cinnamon
1 t. Ginger
1/2 t. Nutmeg
Preheat Oven to 375°
Beat Eggs 5 Minutes. Add Sugar, Pumpkin, & Lemon.
Combine Salt, Flour, Baking Powder, Cinnamon, Ginger,
& Nutmeg. Fold dry ingredients into the mixture.
Line a cookie sheet with parchment paper and spray all of
it with cooking spray. Spread thinly across cookie sheet.
Bake for 15 minutes. While it is still warm, spray
aluminum foil with cooking spray and put on the top and
roll it up length wise. Allow to cool rolled up.

FILLING

1 c. Powdered Sugar
6 oz. Cream Cheese
4 t. Butter
1/2 t. Vanilla
Beat Cream Cheese and Butter until it is smooth.
Add Powdered Sugar and Vanilla.

Unroll cake. Place frosting on cake and reroll.

BREAD PUDDING

4 c. Dried Bread Cubes
2 c. Coarsely Chopped Oreos
5 Eggs-beaten
2 3/4 c. Milk
1/2 c. Sugar
1 T. Vanilla
1 t. Cinnamon

Place Bread and Oreos in an 8x8 pan.
Beat Eggs, Milk, Sugar, Vanilla, and Cinnamon together.
Pour over the the bread and oreos. *Do not mix.
Bake at 350° 40-45 minutes.

Make up 1 3.4 oz box of instant Vanilla Pudding

Match a batch of carmel sauce from page 74.

Cut bread pudding into cubes after it has cooled. Put 8-9
cubes on a plate, top with 1/3 c. Vanilla Pudding and drizzle
with caramel sauce.

> **History:** This was the Steakhouse's Signature Dessert.
> Whenever someone got a free dessert, this was it and
> it was always a hit!

HOT FUDGE SAUCE

1/2 c. Butter	4 c. Sugar
1 c. Corn Syrup	4 t. Cocoa Powder
1-12 oz. Can of	Dash of Salt
Evaporated Milk	1 t. Vanilla

Melt Butter in a heavy sauce pan. Mix Sugar, Salt, and Cocoa Powder in a separate bowl and then add to butter.

Stir in Corn Syrup and then gradually add the Evaporated Milk. Stir Constantly.

Once it boils, continue stirring until sugar is dissolved.

Mix in vanilla and Enjoy!

CARAMEL SAUCE

1 c. Butter	2 1/4 c. Brown Sugar
Dash of Salt	1 c. Corn Syrup
1-15 oz. Can of	1 t. Vanilla
Sweetened	
Condensed Milk	

Melt Butter in a heavy sauce pan.

Add Sugar and Salt. Stir in Corn Syrup and then gradually add the Sweetened Condensed Milk. Stir Constantly.

Once it boils, continue stirring for a few minutes. Mix in vanilla and Enjoy!

SNICKERDOODLE COOKIE

1 c. Room Temperature Butter

1 1/2 c . Sugar

2 Eggs

1 t. Vanilla

1/4 t. Salt

3 c. Flour

1 t. Baking Soda

2 t. Cream of Tartar

Preheat Oven to 350 °

Cream together Butter, Sugar, Eggs, Vanilla, and Salt.

Whisk together Flour, Baking Soda, and Cream of Tartar in a separate bowl.

Gradually add dry ingredients to the mixture. Stop mixing as soon as it comes together.

Mix 4 T of Cinnamon with 2 t. Sugar to roll the dough in.

Scoop into balls.

Roll in Cinnamon/Sugar mixture.

Bake for 10 minutes. Rotate at 5 minutes.

Makes 2 dozen cookies.

PUMPKIN CHOCOLATE CHIP COOKIE

1/2 c. Butter
1/2 c. Sugar
1 1/2 c. Brown Sugar
2 Eggs
1 t. Vanilla
1/2 t. Salt
1 1/2 c. Pumpkin Puree

2 1/2 c. Flour
3/4 t. Baking Soda
1/2 t. Baking Powder
2 t. Pumpkin Pie Spice

3/4 c. Chocolate Chips
1 c. Walnuts

Preheat Oven to 350°
Cream together Butter, Sugars, Eggs, Vanilla, Salt,
and Pumpkin Puree.
Whisk together Flour, Baking Soda, and Baking
Powder, and Pumpkin Pie Spice in a separate bowl.
Gradually add dry ingredients to the mixture.
Then add the Chocolate Chips and Walnuts.
Bake for 18 minutes. Rotate at 9 minutes.
Makes 2 dozen Cookies.

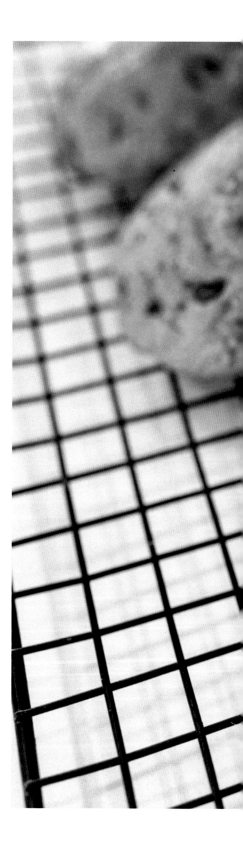

PEANUT BUTTER COOKIE

1/2 c. Butter-Room Temperature

1 c. Peanut Butter

1 c. Brown Sugar

1 c. Sugar

2 Eggs

1 t. Vanilla

1/2 t. Salt

2 1/2 c. Flour

1/2 t. Baking Soda

1 1/2 t. Baking Powder

1/2 c. Milk

Preheat Oven to 350°

Cream together Butters, Sugars, Eggs, Vanilla, and Salt.

Whisk together Flour, Baking Soda, and Baking Powder in a separate bowl.

Gradually add dry ingredients to the mixture.

Add the Milk.

Scoop into Balls then flatten with a fork in a criss cross pattern.

Bake for 10 minutes. Rotate at 5 minutes.

Makes 2 dozen cookies.

OATMEAL COOKIE

1 c. Butter
3/4 c. Brown Sugar
3/4 c. Sugar
2 Eggs
1 1/2 t. Vanilla
1 t. Salt

2 c. Flour
2 c. Oats
1 t. Baking Soda

1 c. Walnuts
1 Package of Milk Chocolate Chips

Preheat Oven to 350°
Cream together Butter, Sugars, Eggs, Vanilla, and Salt.
Whisk together Flour, Oats, and Baking Soda in a
separate bowl.
Gradually add dry ingredients to the mixture.
Then add the Chocolate Chips and Walnuts.
Scoop and Bake for 10 minutes. Rotate at 5 minutes.
Makes 2 dozen cookies.

This is a great recipe to substitute Raisins, if you love an
Oatmeal Raisin Cookie. A favorite is Craisins with
White Chocolate Chips!

SUGAR COOKIE

1/2 c. Butter Room Temperature

1 c. Sugar

1 Egg

1 T. Vanilla

1 t. Salt

3 3/4 c. Flour

2 t. Baking Powder

1 t. Baking Soda

Preheat Oven to 350°.

Cream together Butter, Sugar, Eggs, Vanilla, and Salt.

Whisk together Flour, Baking Powder, and Baking Soda in a separate bowl.

Add gradually to the mixture.

Roll on a floured surface to 1/4 inch thick and cut into desired shape. Place on a cookie sheet.

Bake for 9 minutes. Rotate at 5 minutes.

Let cool completely before frosting.

FROSTING

1/2 c. Butter Room Temperature

1 lb Powdered Sugar

1 t. Vanilla

1 t. Salt

1/4 c. Canned Milk

Cream Butter and then gradually add the Powdered Sugar.

Add in Vanilla, Salt, and Canned Milk to get the perfect frosting consistency.

Makes 2 dozen cookies.

PIE CRUST

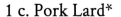

1 c. Pork Lard*
3 c. Flour
1 1/2 t. Salt
2 T. Sugar
1 egg
2 T. Vinegar
4 T. Water

Combine Lard, Flour, Salt, and Sugar until it just starts holding together.
Add Egg, Vinegar, and Water. Mix until it is combined. Don't over work it.

At the Pie Dump they hand rolled every pie! They found the best way is to place about 9 oz of dough in between two large sheets of plastic. Roll it out until it is 1/8 inch thick. Then you can just pull one of the sheets off and place it in the pan. For single crusted pies, Cherie would turn the pie tin upside down and bake it on the outside. She realized that the crusts would shrink a lot less if you baked them that way!

*You can find pork lard in the refrigerated section of most grocery stores. You can also substitute with butter, tallow, coconut oil, or shortening.

History: Most mornings Mac was in baking by 4 am. But on the day before Thanksgiving they would start at midnight and the rest of the staff would join throughout the day. Rolling out 400+ pie crusts was a team effort. Their kids would usually join in baking that day as well and it is a fond memory for them.

87

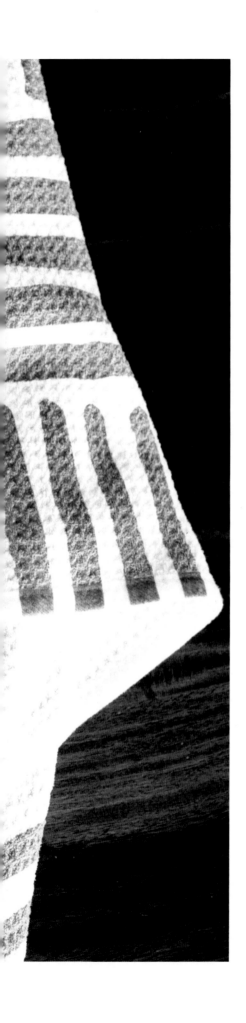

APPLE PIE FILLING

5-6 Granny Smith Apples
1/2 c. Sugar
1 t. Cinnamon
1/4 c. Water
2 T. Cornstarch or 4 T. Flour

Peel, Core, and Slice Apples.
Add Sugar, Cinnamon, Water and either Cornstarch or Flour.
Place in the bottom crust from page 87 and then put the top crust on and decorate the edge as desired.

Bake at 375° for 50 Minutes.

History: To decorate the edges at the Pie Dump, they placed 2 index fingers 1/2 inch apart, gently pressing down around the outside edge of the pie tin. Then push the dough up with a thumb in between index fingers. Pulling the dough around the edge helps the dough from shrinking. Everyone does it a little different, but this is how Mac and Cherie taught it! They also added the cut out heart to every 2 crusted pie as their own little trademark.

PECAN PIE

1/3 c. Butter

1 c. White Karo Syrup

1 c. Brown Sugar

3 Eggs

1 t. Vanilla

1 Heaping Cup Pecan Halves

Preheat Oven to 350°

Prepare pan with pie crust from pg 87.

In a heavy saucepan melt butter. Turn off the heat and add Karo Syrup, Sugar, and Eggs.(Be sure you add your eggs before the mixture gets hot or you will scramble your eggs) Then turn your heat back on to Medium.

Mix and cook until the sugar is dissolved. Add Vanilla.

Add Pecans into prepared pie crust.

With liquid pie fillings sometimes it is easier to place the pie tin on a rack pulled out and pour your ingredients into the crust. Then carefully slide the rack back into the oven.

Bake for 45-50 minutes.

History: Pecan Pies can be a little tricky to get to set up and Cherie admits that in the first years, she didn't always get it right. But she mastered it and occasionally allowed others to help make them. They added the part in the recipe about about scrambling the eggs, because with each new person she taught, they almost always left the heat on and scrambled the eggs on their first time around. Pecan is a family favorite and it is served every year at Thanksgiving!

PUMPKIN PIE

3 Eggs
1 c. Sugar
1/2 t. Salt
1 3/4 t. Pumpkin Pie Spice
1 15 oz can of Pumpkin Puree
1 c. Milk

Preheat Oven to 450°
Beat Egg, Sugar, Salt and Spice together.
Stir in Pumpkin and Milk.
Pour mixture into prepared pie crust from page 87.
With liquid pie fillings sometimes it is easier to
place the pie tin on a rack pulled out and pour your
ingredients into the crust. Then carefully slide the
rack back into the oven.
Bake for 10 minutes.
Reduce heat to 350°. Bake for 40 to 45 minutes.
It is done when a knife inserted in the center
comes out clean. Cool on a wire rack.

History: Pumpkin was, of course, the
Biggest Seller for Thanksgiving! It is a
standard Thanksgiving comfort food!
In the large convection oven they would fill
it with 32 pies over and over again to get all
of the Pumpkin Pies baked.

LEMON MERINGUE PIE

2 c. Water
1 c. Sugar
1 Can of Lemonade Concentrate
1/3 c. Cornstarch
2 Egg Yolks (Save whites for the Meringue)
2 T. Sugar

Combine Water, Sugar, and Concentrate into a saucepan and heat until sugar is dissolved.
Whisk Cornstarch, Eggs, and Sugar together and pour into Lemon Mixture until it thickens.
Pour into your baked crust from page 87 and refrigerate until you are ready to do the Meringue.

MERINGUE

3 Egg Whites
1/2 t. Vanilla
1/4 t. Cream of Tartar
4 T. Sugar

Whip Egg Whites until they are starting to stiffen.
Add Vanilla, Cream of Tartar, and Sugar. Whip until stiff peaks form.
Place on the top of your pie and decorate as desired. Bake at 350° for 12-15 minutes, until the peaks turn golden brown.
This is best done about an hour before you serve it!

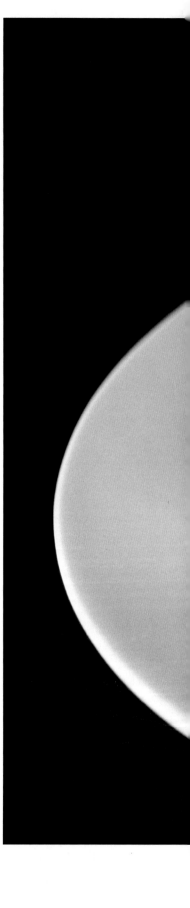

BANANA CREAM PIE

1-3.4 oz Box of Banana Cream Instant Pie/Pudding
2 c. Cold Milk
Whisk Pudding mix into cold milk for 2 minutes. Line your baked and cooled pie crust from page 87 with sliced bananas.*
Put pudding into the pie and refrigerate.
Decorate as desired with whipped cream and more sliced bananas just before serving, so your bananas don't brown.

*Tip: If you are going to make this in the fall or winter, make sure you buy bananas early, because they are often green and take a bit longer to ripen.

History: Cherie would make and bake all the one crusted pies on the Tuesday before Thanksgiving. Then on Wednesday she would make all the fillings and fill all of the one crusted pies. That was something she didn't entrust anyone else to!

Coconut Cream Pie

1-3.4 oz Box of Coconut Cream Instant Pie/Pudding

2 c. Cold Milk

1 c. Shredded Coconut

Whisk Pudding mix into cold milk for 2 minutes. Add in the Coconut.

Put pudding into the baked and cooled pie crust from page 87 and refrigerate.

Decorate as desired with whipped cream and toasted coconut. To toast coconut, cook it for 5-10 minutes on a cookie sheet at 325°. Make sure to stir it every few minutes.

History: Mac and Cherie bought the Pie Dump when they were in the middle of raising their family and having children. The Pie Dump was a second home to the family. In the early years you could find the littlests in a play pen in the back room or in the "rainbow room" in the basement playing or taking naps. Their children went where they did. Once all the kids were in school, Mac would be gone early morning and Cherie would join him as soon as everyone was off to school and they would be home by the time they got home from school. Mac and Cherie were both dedicated to their family and to making The Pie Dump a success.

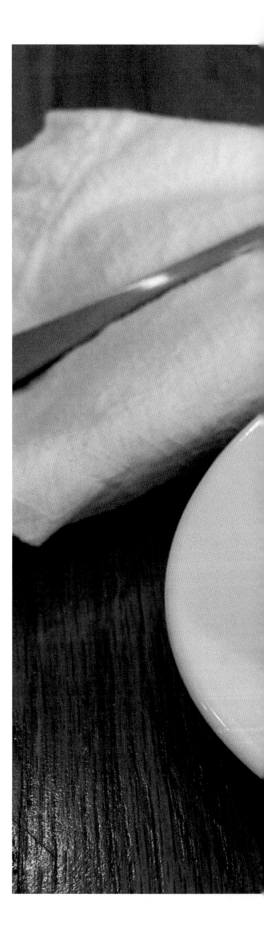

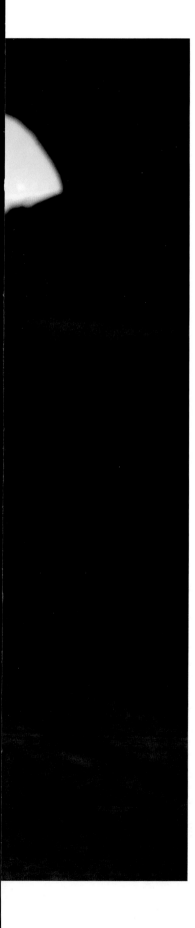

SLUSH

Banana Lemonade

1 can Frozen Lemonade

7 c. Water

2 Blended Bananas

3 c. Simple Syrup(below)

Freeze

Raspberry Lemonade

1 can Frozen Pink Lemonade

7 c. Water

6 oz Raspberries

1 package of Raspberry Flavored Drin kMix

3 c. Simple Syrup(below)

You can add red food coloring to make the color more vibrant.

Freeze.

Orange Pineapple

1-20 oz can of Crushed Pineapple

1 package of Orange Flavored Drink Mix

2 Quarts of Water

3 c. Simple Syrup(below)

Freeze.

Take it out 3 hours before serving. Check it every hour so it doesn't over thaw but you want to be able to stir it.

Simple Syrup

2 c. Water

2 c. Sugar

Place in a sauce pan and boil until sugar is dissolved, then let it cool.

Yields 3 c. of Simple Syrup.

Made in the USA
Las Vegas, NV
02 December 2024

0148d099-0185-4be2-add8-3f98427ae026R01